hey hey pretty baby

philippe shils

right hand pointing

ISBN: 978-1-304-88601-9

Proceeds from the sale of this book benefit the School for Therapeutic and Recreational Riding
3180 S. Mount Zion Rd. Decatur, IL 62521
www.starrfarm.org

The author thanks the editors of these publications for having generously published some of the poems now collected in this chapbook: *Sixth Finch, Hyperlexia Journal, 2River View,* and *elimae*. Much of this material also appears in a web-based chapbook by the same title published on the *right hand pointing* website.

Designed by Dale Wisely.

Cover photo by Philippe Shils.

For more information: righthandpointing@gmail.com

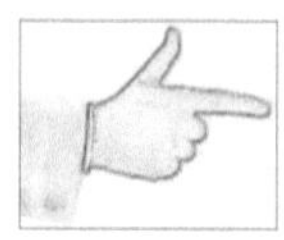

right hand pointing
www.righthandpointing.net

For Lucia of course.
And for the mighty Felix
and the beautiful Amanda.
And with love and thanks
to all the family and friends
who continue to teach
and to be taught by Lucia.

hey hey pretty baby

(high trees)
lucia's barely
freckled
face
turned up
to the
dappled
light
(hi trees)

dry baby

our baby is dry and
we are wringing it against
ourselves trying to wheedle
every bit we can from it

rubbing it against the rocks
of our faces and
wrenching it in our fists

we provoke cajole bite
withhold and taunt
wanting a point a laugh

we beg for a gesture
that means we you or me

something that proves she
deserves to command the dogs

partial complex

1.

there are seizures and the
gasping state just after

this is the tyranny of the hurricane
eyes pulled willy-nilly
and teeth crushed together

there is an absence of grace
here and nothing
that would say
I am making dinner or
I am reciting verse

kissing her head I
feel her soft red hair

2.

if this dissonant
part next to the empty part
of brain were gone
would it go as a vapor
steaming for a moment
then quiet and empty
as the space between planets?
is there a constant

number of souls
in the universe
or is there a constant
wispy mass that makes
up the universe?

Convulsion

surely the pulse from this event
must blow a hard recoil and should
distort my face centrifugally like hers
but the air is still and the neighborhood
quiet   the police will come and
the birds will leap off the branches
and wires   the waters will ripple
and the moon move slightly back
the stars will quiver and the
galaxies shiver for a moment like gongs
this is where all vibrations
should start and maybe do:
in the brain and the nerves and
in the atoms that my daughter shares
with the universe's now discordant timbre

fish and chips with gramps

after we knew
about the stroke
but before the seizures
amanda's father said
I think lucia has
sorted it out.
he'd brought us lunch
and it felt good
to nod and agree.
I knew it was otherwise
and that the damage was
bad and widespread
and too much for
her to overcome.
his optimism
was sweet and
bringing the shell-shocked
their lunch was kind.
we sat in the dining room
eating from styrofoam
and I don't
for the life of me
remember where
lucia was.
the three of us
at the large table
in the heat but

before the
air conditioning
was turned on.

encircled

I've gathered her up
after dinner as
everybody sits
at the cleared table

she spent dinner
in the rocking chair

now my daughter is on my lap
facing me flicking my lapel
saying *dadada*
tatata dat-th dat-th

I hear amanda say
I think maybe
more when he's home
and someone says
she's talking to her daddy

there's no one's eyes I
want to meet but hers
my mouth in the nape
of her neck
her mouth on my ear

our little music we
play at the end
of the table

no cavities

she has no idea
why we're all
peering at her
while her mouth
is held open
and her legs
one arm
and her head
are held still

no cavities
in her perfect teeth

for awhile she
liked nothing
now she's hungry
and likes it all

but still one of her
grandmothers says
this is the only little girl
that doesn't like sweets

halloween is here again
2 weeks after her birthday.
her mother wants to dress
her like a cannoli.

I say *no one*
will know what she is.
her mother says
we'll explain

hey hey pretty baby

woody guthrie's daughter died in a fire
after he wrote her sweet simple songs
and sang them with a plaintive and pleading tone
who's my pretty baby (hey hey pretty baby)

lucia stops at the top of a step or a curb
and as she clutches vaguely for some help
I know that we together lost the mandate of heaven
woody and lucia and cathy and me

a dust bowl and the ceiling fan rhythm
of the locusts that persist all evening

the weather roils on

boiling heat or mean cold

I smell tangerines and taste watermelons

the chill on my tongue
the tang in my nose
and the bitter pleasure of beer

and the rocking of a child
rapid and accelerating
steady and monotonous
and without comfort
frantic and clicking and clacking

lucia's 4th birthday

amanda has a fever of 102.9 today.
is it because lucia is 4 years old today?
how sick will my wife be when lucia is 12?
there have to be circumstances that will
undo the fever and allow us to go to
the park smiling and afebrile.

it's lucia's birthday and she's lying
next to her feverish mother who passed
into delirium 4 years ago.

happy birthday lucia
happiest in the water floating
or held by your mother
in the shower against her breasts
with your head thrown back
or with me gnawing at your
arms and your neck

and the smile atop
your suddenly balanced body
overbalances me.

valentine's day

amanda forgot
this year's
valentine's
day cards.

one of the teachers
said *it's ok.*
it's not
like they know.

amanda confessed
she would have
remembered
if lucia
could understand.

there were 20
little cards
on the kitchen
counter
scattered like
junk mail.

lucia
they said
be mine.

alone with my daughter in the house

when there are leaves
shimmering
she ignores me
preoccupied.

at the window
in the bedroom

the closest she'll get
to a tree house

I have to get in her face
to get a smile.

the winter snow
is something to look
forward to.

we'll be buried
in the neutral light.

indian summer

a coughing wife
sick again and
refusing medicine

windless
the leaves fall
singly

november's
indian summer makes
the windowpanes
warm

the skin of
my daughter's
forehead
is supple
thin and hard

the brain surgeon

said parts
of her brain
would be
like gossamer

and that would
help guide him
to the parts
that are not
like gossamer.

he seemed
competent and
the word gossamer
seemed impractical
and poetic

and I trusted
him then.

visitors

stunned grandparents too old
for this worry and unprepared
for finding their way through the
halls of a children's hospital.
they've dressed nicely and are
unused to feeling so well.
they're more affectionate to one
another than they've been in years.
is this the way he says.
just follow the signs she says
clinging to his arm.

hospital poem

the stitching over
my daughter's left ear
is shaped like a
question mark
the tail of which is
on her temple.
the surgeon told us
this was the way
she would be cut.
I thought he spoke
figuratively but he spoke
literally. they cut her
hair around the incision
and gave it to us
in an envelope.
it's a point of pride to them
that they don't shave
the entire head
and is a comfort
to mothers as well.

co-sleeping

then she dreams and I dream
and she wakes up startled from a dream in which
she follows me into a room and
me from a dream in which
I follow her into a field. a shock passes
through both of us from the ghostly
section of brain which was the part
that would have determined her.

rough play

I gnaw on her. I
won't consume her but I
want to convert her
to our kind.

this is one of the
ways past
her inscrutability.
the opposite
of torture.

today in the snow
she was unhappy
sinking into it.
everything is
solid to her.

we play very rough.
in a lull she perches
on my chin and our
green eyes meet.
maybe we are the
same kind.

untitled

starlings streaming through capillaries
they've found in the sky

when will my head be emptied of verse?

she isn't poetic she is the poem
no poem is about her
she is the poem

I said to my mother
over the phone
my heart is breaking

someday I'll stop seeing
traces of what she
could have been
and see that
she just is

thirsty

because she was crying

I went to the kitchen
to get her some milk.

she shambled into the
kitchen as well maybe

to get some milk. it
was the second time

she's done that so I
only gave her half

so she would be
thirsty again soon.

automatic

I picked up the sugar bowl lid
and took it upstairs
instead of the coffee.

that was something I used to
do in the morning with my
mashed-up thinking and one open eye
but now it happens at night
when I forget the dogs are out
and awaken to barking at 2 a.m.

part of me lives in another dimension
where the milk bottle is a match
and the fork is a baby shoe.

it isn't dementia. it's a preoccupation
with doing what's automatic that
will get worse as she gets older
and the mechanics of every day become
the only way to cope with the drudgery

of the abnormal. the bee flies
to the flower even after its hive is
ablaze and melting. our will to move you
is all there is right now although we

were willing to be moved to a posy
an egg an acorn or a swing with the
freshness and the arc of your leaping voice.

I wake to awaken her

@430 am
the critical hour
between holding it
and going to the bathroom to pee
I give up and walk past lucia's room.
we have a screen door there
so we can see in and it
latches from the outside
so she can't just wander.
I hear the music she plays
by touching a button on a book.
she's laying down
and going back to sleep I think.
I go back to bed and doze.
in her room I find her
in a bunk bed without a top bunk.
I lay beside her and say
I love you lu.
she says
I love you daddy.
I look at my glowing watch
and try to wake myself up
but am unable.
she says *I understand.*
I say *I hear you.*
she seems a genius
because she speaks.

she is sad
old and wise
and consoles me
as I wake to awaken her.

victorian home

I know there is nobility in the
way I'm a father to this child
but I would be reassured by some
sort of celebrity and with my piety
acknowledged. the callous repose
I have with medical talk isn't close
to the agitation she makes me feel and
the bellowing I hope my neighbors
can't hear through the ancient brittle
and rippling windows of our thick
walled and high-ceilinged house.

lucia unweighted

today I took lu swimming.
I had to be convinced by
my wife even though
it's something I've wanted to do.
the y has a shallow warm pool
where old people walk and
children play. there are wheelchairs
in the corner marked with the
floor number of the rehab wing
of the hospital across the street.
lucia was confused by the water
and tried lifting her right leg to the
surface like it was a step.
then she was unweighted.
her right leg rose like it
was made of wood
and she let me lay her
on her back as her neck relaxed.
who could have told me that lucia
can put her head underwater, pause,
blow air out of her mouth and nose,
and surface wet haired and smiling?
nobody, but I knew.

putting a price on her head

the debt collector said
you mentioned your son
and I said *a daughter actually.*
there was silence
and she said *I'll have*
you talk to my manager.
I asked her what there
was that she couldn't explain
and she told me that the
manager would be on
the line soon.
I have to go to work
I said and she said
you called us.
I said *you have*
four minutes
to wind this up miss.
I'll get him she said.
I asked again
what is it that you can't
explain about
what happens next.
the manager came
onto the line and we
wheedled and I accused

him of humiliation
and we came to an agreement.
I said that he must feel
victorious and he told me that
he didn't look at it that way.
I gave him figures then.
that only twenty percent
of people pay their debt
and he conceded that he
was victorious.

the shape of home

she returns to the steps
of the house where we live
even when I walk past
them as a test.
she didn't do it
in the winter.
I've noticed it
this spring.
she must see the slant
of the steps that
sit at an angle
to the sidewalk.
she recognizes the
shape of home.

school picture

in her three-year-old picture
she's on the edge of tears
tense mouthed
gasping and beached

she's in a dress that's
green and orange
and she has a bruise on
her left cheek

she's in a hard chair
maybe for sitting
but not for this fish

she would like to be
underwater where
she came from
and could breathe

she's been
interrupted
repetitively
mouthing coral

survival

about 4 years ago
in the middle of another
of lucia's stupid fucking seizures
I said *I can't take it anymore*
and amanda said
what else are we going to do
what do you want me to say.
and that's how we
survived another day.

my father dreams

my father dreamt
twice last week
that lucia
spoke to him.

I want him to know
that those are
hard dreams
and that I don't want
him to dream them.

rules for writing about lu

never use the word firmament. lucia is earthbound for now. she's all angles not angels. does a bird know it's a bird? does lu know she's lu? I broke my next rule: no questions. we're uncertain if she sings but we know she likes music. don't compare her to a cloud or a flower. don't use the word blessed. I will exile you if you use that fucking word. her hair is red not coppery or golden. anything but golden. she's not related to the sun. she's not akin to light. the word 'inspire' inspires contempt. 'beauty' or 'glow' gets you the guillotine. tell me how unlike her parents she is. and don't flatter her parents; we'll know. she doesn't point; that's fair game. she pushes things away instead of shaking her head. she doesn't understand commerce. find a way to show me that. relating her to brooks, rivers, or streams is unacceptable. be practical. practical would be helpful. I want suggestions not assumptions of grace. realize that when she falls she falls from a high and awkward place. listen to her cry. she cries as though she realizes things about herself that are unwriteable. write about those things.

day one of serial casting

the picture of
a 5-year-old boy
pointing downstream
is more than I
can abide today.

he's in a boat
on a river that runs
through a desert

looking forward
eagerly
his index
finger extended.

home from the stars

this is lucia returned
from the stars

the atoms
she shared
with the
despicable
stars

engulfed in
solar flares
vicious tendrils
whip-cracks

her brain's currents
exposed and flawed

shipwrecker
bonecracker
songscratcher

she's home

candescent

distinct
from the sun

Philippe Shils lives in Decatur, Illinois where he works as a physician assistant. His poems can be read in *Rattle, B O D Y, Right Hand Pointing, Alba, Metazen,* and others. He is a member of the New New Pennies Massive, an online writing workshop. This is his first book. He can be reached at pshils@sbcglobal.net. His website is http://www.philshils.com/

www.ingramcontent.com/pod-product-compliance
Ingram Content Group UK Ltd.
Pitfield, Milton Keynes, MK11 3LW, UK
UKHW041834200726
13854UKWH00003BA/1122